Multiracial Families

THE CHANGING FACE OF MODERN FAMILIES

Multiracial Families

Julianna Fields

Mason Crest Publishers, Inc.

MASON CREST PUBLISHERS INC.
370 Reed Road
Broomall, Pennsylvania 19008
(866)MCP-BOOK (toll free)
www.masoncrest.com

First Printing

9 8 7 6 5 4 3 2 1

ISBN 978-1-4222-1494-7
ISBN 978-1-4222-1490-9 (series)
Library of Congress Cataloging-in-Publication Data
Fields, Julianna.

Produced by Harding House Publishing Service, Inc. www.hardinghousepages.com
Interior Design by MK Bassett-Harvey.
Cover design by Asya Blue www.asyablue.com.
Printed in The United States of America.

Although the families whose stories are told in this book are made up of real people, in some cases their names have been changed to protect their privacy.

Photo Credits

Creative Commons Attribution: D.L. 29, eralon 44, Sam Felder 52, Tracy Hunter 51, inveritaslux 44, kafka4prez 43; GNU Free Documentation License 1.2, Googie Man 13; istockphoto.com: digital skillet 25, spfoto 24

Contents

Introduction

The Gallup Poll has become synonymous with accurate statistics on what people really think, how they live, and what they do. Founded in 1935 by statistician Dr. George Gallup, the Gallup Organization continues to provide the world with unbiased research on who we really are.

From recent Gallup Polls, we can learn a great deal about the modern family. For example, a June 2007 Gallup Poll reported that Americans, on average, believe the ideal number of children for a family to have these days is 2.5. This includes 56 percent of Americans who think it is best to have a small family of one, two, or no children, and 34 percent who think it is ideal to have a larger family of three or more children; nine percent have no opinion. Another recent Gallup Poll found that when Americans were asked, "Do you think homosexual couples should or should not have the legal right to adopt a child," 49 percent of Americans said they should, and 48 percent said they shouldn't; 43 percent supported the legalization of gay marriage, while 57 percent did not. Yet another poll found that 34 percent of Americans feel a conflict between the demands of their professional life and their family life; 39 percent still believe that one parent should ideally stay home with the children while the other works.

Keep in mind that Gallup Polls do not tell us what is right or wrong. They don't report on what people should think—only on what they do think. And what is clear from Gallup Polls is that while the shape of families is changing in our modern world, the concept of family is still vital to our sense of who we are and how we interact with others. An indication of this is the 2008 Gallup poll that found that three out of four Americans reported that family values are important, while one in three said they are "extremely" important.

And how do Americans define "family values"? According to the same poll, here's what Americans say is their definition of a family: a strong unit where faith and morals, education and integrity play important roles within the structure of a committed relationship.

The books in the series demonstrate that strong family units come in all shapes and sizes. Those differences, however, do not change the faith, integrity, and commitment of the families who tell their stories within these books.

1 What Is a Multiracial Family?

Jason's dad is a Baptist with dark brown hair and brown eyes, while his mom is a Catholic with blonde hair and blue eyes.

Sarah's mom was born in Russia, and her dad's family came from England. They're both Jewish.

Scott's father has dark brown skin, and his mother has pale pink skin. Both of them are Christians.

Jennifer's mother is Jewish, while her father is Hindu.

Which of these people would you assume came from multiracial families?

Defining Race

If you said Scott and Jennifer, you'd be like most people who answer this question. The answer come from assumptions that are based on skin color and religion, two factors people often connect with racial differences.

No one notices if a redhead and a blonde get married and have children—but people pay more attention when someone with very dark brown skin has children with someone who has pale skin. A century ago, it was much less common for Catholic communities to intermarry with Protestant; today, we think very little of that, since we do not perceive the two communities as being all that different—but if a Muslim and a Christian marry, we're apt to call it a "multiracial marriage."

What we consider to be the differences between "races," in most cases, are simply physical characteristics, especially skin color, combined with *ethnic* differences, especially religion. The concept of race is simply a way of sorting people into groups.

In reality, however, from a scientific perspective, there is only one "human race." There is no *genetic* basis (nothing in the races' DNA, in other words) that sets one so-called race apart from another. Unlike many animals, human beings have not evolved into subspecies. (Despite our surface differences, we're actually one of the most similar of all species on the Earth.)

Race is not a scientific reality, but it is still an idea that shapes our world. Race opens doors for some peo-

> **Terms to Understand**
>
> ***diversity:*** variety; often referring to groups made up of those with differing characteristics, such as races, religions, cultures, lifestyle practices, etc.
>
> ***stereotypes:*** oversimplified ideas or images held by large numbers of people.
>
> ***biases:*** opinions, prejudices, etc. that prevent a person from considering something objectively.

> Race is a modern idea. Ancient societies did not divide people according to physical differences, but only according to religion, class, or language.

ple—and closes them for others. It allows some groups of people advantages and opportunities that it denies to others. It **generates** laws and policies that make it easier for some people to be educated and get good jobs than for others.

Sociologists believe that the concept or race was born out of slavery. White people used race to justify enslaving certain groups of people; if some people were not truly human—or if they were an inferior form of human being—then it was okay to treat them without dignity. Racial differences were then the justification for taking away Native Americans' land, for excluding Asian immigrants, and for barring Mexican Americans from the same rights as other Americans.

What Do You Think?

Is it hard for you to discuss race openly? Why or why not? As you were growing up, what messages did you learn about race?

Multiracial Families

Multiracial families are created in one of two ways. When two people marry across the racial boundary lines our society has drawn between groups of people, they form a multiracial family. Like all children, theirs will share the genetic characteristics of both their parents; our society may refer to them as mixed-race. And if parents adopt across the racial lines, they also form a multiracial family.

Multiracial children are one of the fastest growing segments of the U.S. population. The number of mixed-race families in America is steadily increasing, due to a rise in interracial marriages and relationships, as well

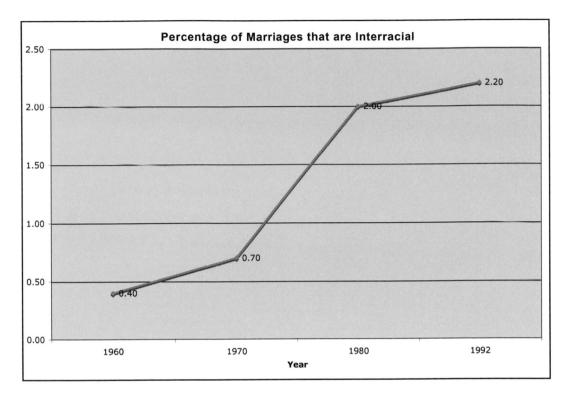

Percentage of Marriages that are Interracial

The number of interracial marriages in the United States has been steadily increasing since 1967 when the U.S. Supreme Court overturned interracial marriage bans. According to a Stanford University study, the number of interracial married couples was up to seven percent by 2005.

as an increase in *transracial* and international adoptions. Publicity surrounding prominent Americans of mixed cultural heritage, such as athletes, actors, musicians, and politicians, has brought the issues these individuals face to society's attention and challenged many of our *prejudices*.

If you picked any two people from Japan and any two people from Nigeria, the Japanese people would be as genetically different from each other as they were from the Nigerian people—and vice versa.

11

Did You Know?

Each society defines race a little differently. According to the U.S. Census, there are 5 races that live in the United States:

1. **White:** People having origins in any of the original peoples of Europe, the Middle East, or North Africa
2. **Black or African American:** People having origins in any of the black racial groups of Africa
3. **American Indian and Alaska Native:** People having origins in any of the original peoples of North and South America (including Central America), and who maintain tribal affiliation or community attachment.
4. **Asian:** People having origins in any of the original peoples of the Far East, Southeast Asia, or the Indian subcontinent.
5. **Native Hawaiian and other Pacific Islander:** People having origins in any of the original peoples of Hawaii, Guam, Samoa, or other Pacific Islands.

Growing Up in a Multiracial Family

"Think of the children," used to be the warning used to discourage interracial couples from marrying. Mixed-race children often faced *discrimination* and prejudice. A "biracial" child, for instance, the offspring of both a black and a white parent, might be rejected by both the black and white communities. Experts worried that these children would suffer from poor self-esteem and a lack of identity.

Society is changing, though. Recent research has shown that multiracial children don't differ from other children in self-esteem or number of psychiatric problems. What's more, these kids tend to be high achievers with a strong sense of self and **tolerance** of **diversity**. In fact, there seems to be some definite advantages to growing up in a multiracial family.

Sociologists (the experts that study society) say that parents of multiracial children tend to think more about cultural heritage. They work to preserve the richness of the customs and languages of both cultures, and in the process, they teach their children to accept differences. Because society still fails to accept these children from time to time, their parents must teach them how to cope with injustice and insult. They learn to confront hostility and curiosity in positive ways.

Derek Jeter, a successful Major League Baseball player, is the child of an interracial marriage—his father is African American and his mother is white, of Irish/German descent.

These families act as bridges between groups of people that were once totally divided by the lines of race. They break the *stereotypes* that have lived for centuries in people's heads. They give us all proof that the so-called races can live together—not only in the same neighborhood but in the same home.

Both Tiger Woods and President Barack Obama are famous children of interracial marriages. Tiger even coined the word Cablinasian (Caucasian, Black, Indian, Asian) to represent his mixed cultural heritage.

Statistics for Multiracial Families

(From U.S. Census 2000)

- Nearly 7 Million (2.4 percent) of Americans described themselves as multiracial in the 2000 Census.
- The number of interracial couples more than quadrupled between 1970 and 1995. In the United States marriages between blacks and whites increased 400 percent in the last 30 years, with a 1000 percent increase in marriages between whites and Asians.
- About two million American children have parents of different races.

The Research Says . . .

- Children in a multiracial family often have different racial identities from one another; in other words, one sibling may think of himself as black, while another identifies as white. Their racial identities will be influenced by their individual physical features, family attachments and support (whether they're closer to Mom or Dad), and their experiences with racial groups.

There are approximately 7 million people in the United States who identify as mixed-race, with half of these being under the age of 18. It is estimated that the mixed-race population in the U.S. will reach 21% by 2050.

- To cope with society's *biases*, mixed-race children may develop a public identity with the "minority" race, while maintaining a private interracial identity with family and friends. This means that at school, a young person might act and talk like a black kid—while at home, she thinks of herself as someone who is not defined by race.
- Research has shown that children with a truly multiracial or multicultural identity generally grow up to be happier than multiracial children who grow up with a "single-race" identity.
- Multiracial children in divorced families may have greater difficulties accepting and valuing the cultures of both parents.

HEADLINES

(From *St. Louis Beacon*, Kristen Hare, "Obama's Example Helps Multiracial Individuals in Effort to Claim Their Full Identities, January 16, 2009. © 2009 by St. Louis Beacon)

This fall during the presidential election, Harper Grace Biley sat with her mother, watching TV, when a commercial came on.

"Mommy, look," B.J. Biley remembers her daughter saying. "A-rock Obama is brown like me."

"I said, 'You bet he is, and he's also running for president of the United States,'" Biley says.

"Well, I bet his mommy is really proud of him," Harper Grace told her mom.

"And I said, 'Yes baby, she is.'"

The 4-year-old from Blue Springs, Mo., could see that the future president was biracial, both white and black, like her. And like her, his maternal grandparents were also white.

When people ask, Harper Grace explains that she's brown—easier, her mom thinks, than saying biracial, but just as descriptive. . . .

. . . Most people know someone who is multiracial or multiethnic. It's not such a big deal, really. The problem, says the executive director for the Center for the Study of Biracial Children, is that academia and the government are 30 or 40 years behind, still wanting people to choose one identity.

The media don't get off easy, either.

"In general," he says, "if a multiracial person is involved in something negative, they always point out that they're multiracial." If that person's getting good press, he says, there's often just one race mentioned. But the reality that most people seem to accept, he adds, is that people are allowed to be more than one thing.

A FEW FAMOUS MIXED-RACE INDIVIDUALS
Barack Obama
Cameron Diaz
Alicia Keys
Paula Abdul
Jimi Hendrix
Dwayne Johnson
(the Rock)
Tiger Woods

In a recent survey, 47% of white teens, 60% of black teens, and 90% of Hispanic teens said they had dated someone of another race.

In the 2000 Census, 6.8 million people, or 2.4 percent of the population, identified themselves as more than one race. That option isn't available to parents or students in Missouri schools, however.

Sharnell Sharp, now 19 and a sophomore at the University of Missouri St. Louis, is the daughter of a Mexican-American mom and a black dad. Sharp grew up in a black neighborhood, went to a mostly black school, but knew her mom's ethnicity was a part of her, as well.

Her identity never seemed a huge issue, however, until high school, when Sharp was taking a state test. Under race, she was told she had to check one box, black. "And I couldn't understand why, because I was both and I wanted to mark 'other.'"

And the category African American, non-Hispanic didn't work, either.

Sharp put up a fight. "I'm mixed with both," she says. "It's 50/50 for both. So I shouldn't have to choose one or the other. It's not fair to me."

That's the same point that drives the work behind Project Race. The nonprofit was founded in 1991 and has changed legislation for multiracial classification in Ohio, Illinois, Georgia, Indiana, Michigan and Maryland, as well as several cities in other states.

Harper Grace's mom became a member of the group after her husband was told he had to check just one box when registering their son for school, according to Missouri Department of Education guidelines. If they didn't mark one box, they were told, a member of the staff would observe their son and choose one for him.

That seemed unfair to the Bileys, and now they're working with their state legislator, Rep. Bryan Pratt, to have multiracial classification legislation passed in Missouri. . . .

So what's the big deal, really? If a child has to mark a box that doesn't represent who they are, where's the harm?

"Identity, identity, identity," Graham says. "We all come from different places . . . it's being able to embrace a person's entire heritage. That's important."

And the ability to embrace that heritage is changing, too.

Wardle and Graham both say biracial and multiracial people of past generations have felt the need to pick one culture over the other.

No more, they say, and that reflects the expanding and connected world younger generations now live in.

MORE STATISTICS

Thirty years ago, only one in every 100 children born in the United States was of mixed race. Today that number is one in 19. In states like California and Washington it's closer to one in 10.

"They're multi everything," Wardle says. "We have a generation of people who say, '[Forget] this whole thing, it doesn't make sense.'". . .

Usually, when people ask Paige Overton, 8, of Wentzville, about her ethnicity, they guess completely wrong.

Paige's mom, Tracy, is white, and her dad, Jerry, is black.

For the most part, Paige's mom isn't concerned about how her daughter and son identify themselves. They're both black and white. They spend time with both cultures, live in a multiracial neighborhood and attend a multiracial school in Wentzville.

And those things are key for raising successful multiracial children, Wardle says.

"Saying you have the best of both worlds is absolutely meaningless," he says.

Instead, multiracial kids need to experience it, to have role models in both and a clear and easy term for what they are, so that when people ask, they're ready. . . .

What Do You Think?

Do you think it's important to use and understand the term "multiracial" when speaking of people who come from many different heritages? Why or why not? Do you think our society will ever get to the point where we no longer pay any more attention to "race" than we do to eye color or hair color? Why or why not?

2 Multiracial Adoption

In the wilds of Pennsylvania is a rambling house with a gigantic yard. Three children—two brothers and a sister—have created hills and valleys all over the land. It's a skateboard and snowboard heaven, and they keep their adopted father busy building ramps that serve as the props for daredevil feats in every season. In winter they also cross-country ski through the woods and fields or roar through well-used trails on their snowmobiles. In summertime they take to the creek, where they can swim and fish and stay cool no matter how hot the day.

These three siblings are living in far different circumstances than those in which their parents grew up.

Their mother, Sheena Jones, met their father, Lemuel Simpson, at their school in

Philadelphia, in one of the toughest and poorest parts of the city. Sheena was only fourteen when she found out she was carrying a baby. A year after Marvin was born, she discovered she was pregnant again—but this time it was twins.

She wanted to stay in school, but she knew she couldn't handle it with three children. So she went to a

According to the Child Welfare Information Gateway, there were an estimated 510,000 children in foster care. Of this 510,000, 53% are reunited with parents or family, 17% are adopted, 16% go to live with a relative, 9% are emancipated and 4% have some other outcome.

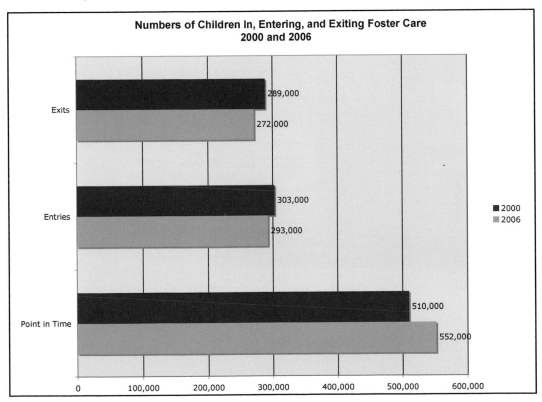

Parents with multiracial children may have concerns that other parents do not have, such as how to include unfamiliar cultural traditions in their children's lives.

social services agency, which helped her with the paperwork to put Marvin and the two new babies, once they were born, into the *foster-care system*.

Meanwhile, Floyd and Flora Webber were cleaning out the last boxes from their three children, who now had homes and children of their own. They thought the time might have come for them to downsize, to sell their big house surrounded by woods in rural Pennsylvania and move into a smaller place in the city. After all, Floyd had retired and didn't really want to spend all his time mowing a two-acre lawn. Flora was tired of dusting and vacuuming the four-bedroom house and taking care of her big vegetable garden. They were both nearly sixty. Maybe they could take a cruise or visit Hawaii, if they could sell the house and leave behind that whole set of heavy and relentless responsibilities.

Then their daughter called. As a social worker in Philadelphia, she had come upon a sad situation, she told them. Three baby siblings had nowhere to go. The foster care system was overflowing with unwanted children. "By any chance did you ever consider starting a second family?" she asked her parents.

Floyd and Flora sank into their respective armchairs after the call. A second family? No, they had never once considered the idea.

But should they?

After all, they had a suitable house, lived in an area with good schools, and had plenty of love in their hearts to share. Maybe they shouldn't be selfish—

Their conversation was interrupted when the phone rang again—and again it was their daughter. "By the way," she said, "I forgot to tell you, but the babies are black."

Floyd and Flora were of German heritage and with skin as white as it could be.

Did that make any difference? they asked themselves. Neither one had been brought up with people of other cultures. Not that they were prejudiced—but they had never been exposed to African American people. Did the children's parents have different *traditions* from their own? Would they be doing the children a *disservice* when they were so ignorant of their **ethnic heritage**? Would people in the black community feel that the children should be raised by others within the same community, instead of by two old white folks?

Color didn't matter to them, they decided, but they still worried that it might be unfair to bring up Marvin,

A child whose parents are of different ethnicities faces a different set of challenges than an adopted child. She may struggle with how to identify her ethnicity and therefore herself.

Monique, and Milton in a rural county that, as far as they knew, had no other people of color in it.

But where would these children go if the Webbers couldn't take them? Would they be pulled apart and bumped around the foster care system their entire lives?

So Floyd hauled out his paintbrush and roller, and Flora started refinishing cribs and dressers. Soon their house was full of the noise of a busy family again.

Neighbors gossiped about the Webbers' decision to adopt when they were no longer young anymore. Some said their actions were noble; others thought they were taking on too much and they'd regret it. Everybody had an opinion—and that was before the babies arrived. When three children with curly black hair and dark skin arrived, phone lines buzzed all around the county.

But when a crowd of neighbors descended on the Webbers' doorstep, bearing toys and clothes and gifts for the little newcomers, it was clear these children would be accepted in the community.

By the time the adoption papers were signed, the siblings were two and three years old. Their mother had met the Webbers only once, but their father planned to visit the children at least once or twice a year.

When Marvin started kindergarten, he met with only one bully who decided to call him names. Their teacher straightened the child out quickly and sent him and Marvin to play a game together.

So **assimilation** was easy—from the point of view of everybody, that is, but the ones who counted most: Marvin, Monique, and Milton.

As they got older, it bothered them more and more that they didn't look like anybody around them. Their hair didn't behave the way other kids' did. When their **biological** father visited, he seemed angry that they didn't know anything about rap music or musicians. They felt like they were letting him down, and they wondered where they really belonged.

Flora talked with her daughter about the kids' problems, who invited the family to come to Philly. There the boys went to a barber who knew how to cut their hair, and Monique visited a beautician who specialized in cornrows. Flora's daughter and a friend took the kids out shopping for urban-style clothes and a few CDs. The kids came back home having seen a whole new world, abounding with faces that looked like theirs—and they wanted to see more of it.

Their push for independence—which most children **initiate** sooner or later—had begun early. This time the Webbers weren't sure how to cope with the growing rebelliousness of the children.

When the siblings reached adolescence, their father approached Floyd and Flora and asked if he could take the kids to his home in Philly for a week in the summer. He wanted to show them his way of life, he told them. Nervously, they agreed. Being exposed to African-

American city life was one thing the Webbers couldn't provide.

So the children grew into teenagers, spending a week every summer with their father in Philly and living in a totally white rural world the rest of the time.

At school, they were called upon to set up Kwanzaa displays. "What's Kwanzaa?" they asked.

Rap and hip hop are an important part of African American urban culture. African American children raised in a mostly white, rural community will miss out on this aspect of their heritage unless they are exposed to it via city visits.

They felt tugged between their father and the Webbers, between one culture and another, one race and another. Where did they really belong?

When they went off to college, though, they discovered they didn't have to choose. Students of all colors and cultures lived in the dormitories, and within that mix, the three siblings found themselves very much at home.

Today, as young adults, the Webbers offer the world a very important bridge between two very separate worlds. Their upbringing may have been challenging in some ways, but unlike most of us, they have had the opportunity to truly understood two very different cultural worlds, from the inside out.

What Do You Think?

If you were the Webber children, how would you have felt growing up in an all-white community? Do you think Floyd and Flora did the right thing by adopting the children? Why or why not? If people from the same ethnic background live together in the same community, what are the advantages to the community members—and what are the disadvantages? Do you think Floyd and Flora's age may have affected their ability to be on the "same wavelength" as their

children as much as the color of their skin?
Why or why not?
Why do you think the author would say our world
needs "bridges" like the Webber children?

HEADLINES

(From ANI, "Brad Pitt: Our Multiracial Brood," Rajesh, January 10, 2009.)

Brad Pitt might be raising six kids from four different countries, but the Hollywood star insists that they are bound by blood.

Pitt and partner Angelina Jolie, have three biological kids Shiloh, Knox and Vivienne, and three adopted Maddox, Zahara and Pax.

"It is chaos in moments but there is such joy in the house," *The Sun* quoted him as telling *Total Film.*

"I look down and there is our boy from Vietnam, our daughter from Ethiopia, our girl born in Namibia and our son from Cambodia and they are brothers and sisters, man, they are blood," he added.

And the couple still plans to adopt.

The *Fight Club* star insists that they have "not found any reason" to stop adopting.

What Do You Think?

Do you Brad Pit and Angelina Jolie's children will grow up thinking of their family as multiracial? Why or why not? Do feel that these celebrity parents should continue to adopt more children? Why or why not?

HEADLINES

(From "Raising Katie," by Tony Dokoupil, *Newsweek Web*, Apr. 23, 2009.)

Several pairs of eyes follow the girl as she pedals around the playground in an affluent suburb of Baltimore. But it isn't the redheaded fourth grader who seems to have moms and dads of the jungle gym nervous on this recent Saturday morning. It's the African-American man—six feet tall, bearded and wearing a gray hooded sweatshirt—watching the girl's every move. Approaching from behind, he grabs the back of her bicycle seat as she wobbles to a stop. "Nice riding," he says, as the fair-skinned girl turns to him, beaming. "Thanks, Daddy," she replies. The onlookers are clearly flummoxed.

As a black father and adopted white daughter, Mark Riding and Katie O'Dea-Smith are a sight at best surprising, and at worst so perplexing that people feel compelled to respond. Like the time at a Pocono Mountains flea market when Riding scolded Katie, attracting so many sharp glares that he and his wife, Terri, 37, and also African-American, thought "we might be lynched." And the time when well-intentioned shoppers followed Mark and Katie out of the mall to make sure she wasn't being kidnapped. Or when would-be heroes come up to Katie in the cereal aisle and ask, "Are you OK?"—even though Terri is standing right there.

Is it racism? The Ridings tend to think so, and it's hard to blame them. To shadow them for a day, as I recently did, is to feel the unease, notice the negative attention and realize that the same note of fear isn't in the air when they attend to their two biological children, who are 2 and 5 years old. It's fashionable to say that the election of Barack Obama has brought the dawn of a post-racial America. . . .

. . . But the Ridings' experience runs counter to these popular notions of harmony. And adoption between races is particularly fraught. So-called transracial adoptions have surged since 1994, when the Multiethnic Placement Act reversed decades of outright racial matching by banning discrimination against adoptive families on the basis of race. But the growth has been all one-sided. The number of white families

adopting outside their race is growing and is now in the thousands, while cases like Katie's—of a black family adopting a nonblack child—remain frozen at near zero. . . .

. . . African-Americans can also be wary when one of their own is a parent to a child outside their race. Just ask Dallas Cowboys All-Pro linebacker DeMarcus Ware and his wife, Taniqua, who faced a barrage of criticism after adopting a nonblack baby last February. When *The New York Times* sports page ran a photo of the shirtless new father with what appeared to be a white baby in his arms (and didn't mention race in the accompanying story), it sent a slow shock wave through the African-American community, pitting supporters who celebrated the couple's joy after three painful miscarriages against critics who branded the Wares "self-race-hating individuals" for ignoring the disproportionate number of blacks in foster care. The baby, now their daughter, Marley, is in fact Hispanic. "Do you mean to tell me that the Wares couldn't have found a little black baby to adopt?" snarled one blogger on the *Daily Voice*, an online African-American newspaper.

For the relatively few black families that do adopt non-African-American children, and the adoptive children themselves, the experience can be confusing. "I hadn't realized how often we talked about white people at home," says Mark. "I hadn't realized that dinnertime stories were often told with reference to the race of the players, or that I often used racial stereotypes, as in the news only cares about some missing spring–break girl because she is blonde.'"

Katie, too, has sometimes struggled with her unusual situation, and how outsiders perceive it. When she's not drawing, swimming or pining after teen heart-throb Zac Efron, she's often dealing with normal kid teasing with a nasty edge. "They'll ignore me or yell at me because I have a black family," she says. Most of her friends are black, although her school is primarily white. And Terri has noticed something else: Katie is uncomfortable identifying people by their race.

Is she racially confused? Should her parents be worried? Opinions vary in the larger debate about whether race is a legitimate consideration in adop-tion. At present, agencies that receive public funding are forbidden from taking race into account when screening potential parents. . . .

. . . The Ridings, for their part, are taking Katie's racial training into their own hands. They send her to a mixed-race school, and mixed-race summer camps, celebrate St. Patrick's Day with gusto and buy Irish knickknacks, like a "Kiss Me I'm Irish" T shirt and a mug with Katie's O'Dea family crest emblazoned on

it. But they worry it won't be enough. "All else being equal, I think she should be with people who look like her," says Mark. "It's not fair that she's got to grow up feeling different . . . ."

What Do You Think?

Would Katie O'Dea-Smith be better off if she'd been adopted by a white family? Why or why not? How important is race to *your* identity?

3 Intermarriage

When she was a child, Venu Singh's parents spoke to her in their native Hindi, but they demanded that she answer them in the language of their new land, America. Her father was a professor at a local college as well as a researcher, and he expected his five children to go to college, succeed in whatever profession they chose—and to stay true to the faith and heritage of their ancestors.

Statues of Hindu deities filled their home. Her devoted parents, who had **emigrated** from India, would lay food at the statues' feet. Venu watched, confused and troubled her that the gods never consumed the food given to them.

Although her family had been Hindu for as far back as anyone could remember, Venu began to question the **tenets** of that faith. By the time she was in high school, her curiosity compelled her to

Terms to Understand

ordination: the ceremony by which a person is granted a position of ministry in the Christian church.
Messianic: related to the Messiah, the expected deliverer of the Jewish people, who, in Christian belief, is Jesus Christ.
incorporate: include, unite.
heritage: something that comes to a person by way of their birth.

investigate other religious traditions. She explored the various forms of Christianity introduced to her by friends.

She discovered that some Christian church services were silent and *reverential*, while others were noisy and *boisterous*. Venu came to understand that a wide *spectrum* of attitudes and practices were *encompassed* within the word "Christianity."

She delved into Judaism, too, and found the same breadth of differences.

What Is Hinduism?

Hinduism, the predominant religion of the Indian subcontinent, believes in many gods, with Vishnu and Shiva being among the most popular deities. Reincarnation, karma, and personal duty, or dharma, are all important Hindu concepts. It is the Earth's oldest living religion, formed from many different traditions and with no single founder (such as Christianity's Jesus or Islam's Mohammed). Hinduism is the world's third largest religion (after Christianity and Islam), with approximately a billion adherents, of whom about 905 million live in India. Other countries with large Hindu populations can be found across southern Asia.

What Is Christianity?

Christianity centers on the life and teachings of Jesus of Nazareth as presented in the New Testament Scripture. Christians call Christ's message of love and salvation for all humanity the Gospel ("good news").

Christianity began as a Jewish sect in the eastern Mediterranean. It quickly grew in size and influence over a few decades. Christianity has played a prominent role in the shaping of Western civilization at least since the fourth century. As of the early 21st century, Christianity has between 1.5 billion and 2.1 billion adherents, representing about a quarter to a third of the world's population. It is the world's largest religion.

Some more modern Jewish groups permitted females to become *rabbis*; others did not even allow women to sit near men in the synagogue.

She read novels by Rabbi Chaim Potok and she found herself intrigued by the world of *ultra-orthodox* Hasidic Judaism. In that tradition, men with long earlocks (curls of hair grown from their temples) cover themselves with four-cornered fringed garments when they pray and wear yarmulkes (special hats) on their heads at all other times; both practices show respect and submission to

What Do Jews Believe?

Judaism is a set of beliefs and practices originating in the Hebrew Bible (referred to as the "Old Testament" by Christians). It is based on the relationship between the Children of Israel (later, the Jewish nation) and God. It is considered either the first or one of the first monotheistic (one-god) religions, and it is among the oldest religious traditions still being practiced today.

God, the Master of the Universe. Women lived under strict rules that guided their every action and attitude.

Venu was captivated by the depth and *rituals* of Hasidism, but ultimately, that faith did not win her heart. She decided to commit herself to Christianity.

By now she was an adult, living a thoroughly American life. She had graduated from college and became a teacher. In the eyes of her *conservative* parents, she should still be a respectful daughter, ready to listen and accept their council. But she horrified them when she explained that she would not accept an arranged marriage within their religious tradition, although they fully expected her to let them choose a husband for her.

What Is Hasidic Judaism?

Hasidic Judaism (from a Hebrew word that means "piety" or "loving kindness") is a type of Orthodox Jewish religious movement. The movement originated in Eastern Europe (what is now Ukraine) in the eighteenth century, and soon spread from Poland and Russia, to Hungary and Romania. As compared with other Jewish movements, Hasidic Judaism tends to focus on the role of the Rebbe (or Rabbi) as God's spiritual messenger. Hasidic followers join worship groups associated with dynasties of Hasidic spiritual leaders. Each dynasty follows its own principles; this means that Hasidic Judaism is not one movement, but a collection of separate individual groups with some things in common. There are some nine major Hasidic groups, approximately thirty smaller Hasidic groups, and several hundred minor or extinct Hasidic groups. Though there is no one single version of Hasidism, individual Hasidic groups often share with each other a fundamental philosophy, worship styles, dress, and songs. They also share the belief that every act and word of human beings produces a corresponding effect in the upper spheres. Because of this, they cling to God in order to unite with the source of life and then influence it. This communion is achieved through concentrating their thoughts on God, and consulting him in all of life's affairs.

Venu believed God would find a suitable mate for her, and that the man would be indicated to her when he used the words, "I feel you're to be my wife."

When a tall man named Ron Goldberg spoke those very words a short time later, she confidently agreed to marry him—even though the two of them were relative strangers when they exchanged their vows.

Ron, whose ancestors had lived in America for generations, had been brought up an observant Jew. At age thirteen he had celebrated his Bar Mitzvah, a coming-of-age ceremony where he consciously and publicly accepted the faith. But as the years passed he, too, ventured beyond the bounds of his family's belief system.

Ultimately he converted to Christianity, but without shunning the traditions of his family's Jewish heritage. He accepted *ordination* as a Christian minister as well as a *Messianic* rabbi. When asked to explain his faith, he says that he believes Jesus to be the Messiah, but that Judaism remains his culture. Now he serves two congregations, one Messianic and one long-established Christian, in the same rural church building.

On Saturdays—the Jewish Sabbath—he blows his shofar, a traditional instrument used to gather Jewish congregations together, and addresses the group gathered for a "Mashiach Yisrael" service. Wearing a yarmulke, Messianic Rabbi Ron quotes the Torah while the women of the church dance in the aisles.

They sing songs in Hebrew while he plays the melody on the piano.

Then on Sundays—the Christian Sabbath—he appears at the same podium again, this time as Pastor

Hasidic Judaism is a type of Orthodox Judaism. As such, marriage to a person of another faith is forbidden, and seen as a rejection of Judaism.

Ron, minister to the assembled congregation of Christian Missionary and Alliance believers. This time they sing in English as he accompanies them on the same keyboard.

Both groups learn about the context of biblical times from a man who is well-versed in ancient history, and

Each culture celebrates marriage with a unique ceremony—shown here are a Jewish ceremony (left) and an Indian ceremony (right). Sometimes an interfaith couple will choose to hold two ceremonies—one to celebrate each cultural tradition.

to both he delivers essentially the same spiritual messages. In return, both congregations respect him and appreciate the community outreach to which he inspires them. He set up a Web site, jewishjesus.org, in which he put his quirky sense of humor to work. In headings such as "Have Shofar Will Travel," he indicates his willingness to bring his multicultural teachings to other congregations.

Today, he and Venu are the parents of five children: Ravi, Caleb, Asha, Reva and Gita—their mother's Asian ancestry evident in their names. Venu homeschooled them all until the youngest turned eight years old. Their home is a melting pot of cultures, one that's always open to others of any faith and any background.

Venu has thrived in the multiracial, multiethnic, multi-religion household that she and Ron have created. She is a solid supporter of her husband and a quiet but strong leader of the women in both congregations, as well as a positive influence to many local children. Her parents have come to slowly accept her choices. They see that she has a good home and a secure life, and they cannot fault the care and guidance she showers on their grandchildren. She melds Indian and American, as well as Jewish and Christian, traditions within its walls. Ron says she's a great cook, preparing the foods on which she was raised. The children love her curry with the bread called roti.

"We try to find ways to *incorporate* her *heritage* into our clothing and food," he explains. "She has several Indian outfits, and I love the Indian suit they got me."

Venu regrets that she has forgotten much of the Hindi language she learned as a child, but she wants to give her children at least a passing familiarity with it. They all speak English and can also at least recognize some Hebrew letters. The family celebrates both Christmas and Hannukah, dubbing it "Christmakah," with both a decorated Christmas tree and a gleaming menorah.

The Goldbergs are a living example that races and religions can thrive together, not only side-by-side but blended, each benefiting from the other.

What Do You Think?

Some people might feel that by combining so many traditions, the Goldbergs have failed to be true to any of them; that by being so many things at once, they've actually abandoned their unique ancient heritages. What do you think?

As racial communities mix together more and more, do you think families like the Goldbergs will become more common? Why or why not? In what ways do you think race and religion are connected?

HEADLINES

(From "Obama and America's 'Patchwork Heritage,'" by Jennifer Brea, CNN, January 21, 2009.)

When I was a small child, even before I had the right vocabulary, I could tell that my parents were different.

When I was with my mother, strangers would gush over me. When I was with my father, I felt a distance.

For reasons deeper than I could explain, it was safer with Mom; I was more special when, as far as the outside world could see, I belonged to her.

I later learned this was because people were reacting to the fact that my mother was white and my father black. Like a growing number of Americans, like our new president, I grew up straddling this country's racial divisions. . . .

Tiger Woods, when he rose to fame as America's first black golf star, caused an uproar after he told reporters he was "Cablinasian," a nod to his Caucasian, Black, Native American and Asian ancestry. (He is one quarter African–American.) . . .

The story of my own family was similarly complex. My Anglo-Irish mother is as white as they come. But my father is Haitian, the descendant of West African

slaves and French plantation owners, as well as Chinese and Egyptian. And still, growing up, I was asked to choose between one of the two boxes available to me. "Are you black or are you white?"

It took until 2000 before the U.S. Census allowed respondents to check off more than one racial category, a formal recognition that there are no longer two Americas, one black, one white, but dozens, maybe hundreds, of overlapping Americas.

By [Obama] telling his story of being raised by white grandparents in Hawaii, their love for him and his grandmother's utterance of racial stereotypes, and his adult quest to connect to his father's Kenyan roots, Obama has changed the entire dialogue about race.

He has managed to accomplish something truly rare: to both carry the mantle of African-Americans' struggle for justice and to transcend it. He is as much the fulfillment of more than 300 years of struggle as he is a symbol of the future: A president who embodies the changing landscape of our imperfect union.

. . . In his inaugural address, Obama said, ". . .our patchwork heritage is a strength, not a weakness. We are a nation of Christians and Muslims, Jews and Hindus—and nonbelievers. We are shaped by every language and culture, drawn from every end of this Earth; and because we have tasted the bitter swill of civil war and segregation, and emerged from that dark chapter stronger and more united, we cannot help but believe that the old hatreds shall someday pass; that the lines of tribe shall soon dissolve. . . ."

When Obama took the stage at Grant Park in Chicago, Illinois, on election night, with his family, it was the first time in my 26 years of living I felt like America really belonged to people like me.

. . . Before we become a "post-racial" America, we have to become one that is truly multiracial, comfortable with the fact that more and more Americans no longer wear their identities on their skins. . . .

What Do You Think?

What did President Obama mean when he said, "that the lines of tribe shall soon dissolve"? Do you think that the author is right when she says that America needs to become a place where people "no longer wear their identities on their skins"?

4 Growing Up Between Two Races

Chakori Redstreet has two white parents, two brown sisters, and a white brother. She and her two younger sisters, Daya and Prisha, were born in India. Chakori can remember the time when they lived in India, but Daya and Prisha have no memories of anything before the life they lead today. Daya was two years old, and Prisha only a baby when they were adopted and came to the United States to be members of the Redstreet family.

"But even though they don't really remember," Chakori says, "I've told them so many stories that they get mixed up and think that my memories are theirs. Even my little brother insists he remembers the orphanage."

Chakori was a five-year-old when her mother died, leaving behind her three little girls. "She was very beautiful," Chakori says. "I remember the colors of her saris, the way they felt against my cheek, the way she smelled. I used to like to put my finger on her _bindi_, the little jewel she wore in the middle of her forehead to remind her that she was blessed. She would crush rose petals and draw bindis on my forehead and on the girls'."

According to a 2007 UNICEF report there are an estimated 25,000,000 orphans in India.

Food is one of the basic facets of every culture. Learning to cook their traditional foods can help adopted children connect with their culture.

Once their mother died, little Chakori became responsible for her baby sisters. Their father worked during the day, leaving the little girls alone. But Chakori remembers very little of this sad time. "The next thing I really remember is the orphanage. I thought it was a very white place. I was used to the colors of my mother's clothes, to marigolds and dirt and fruit everywhere. And that's what I remember first—crying for my mother and staring at everything white. There was white tile on the floor and white beds and white walls, and the sisters all wore white. But later, it didn't seem like that. The sisters were nice, and there was just as many flowers and fruit and dirt there as there had been before. It was my job to help the sisters take care of my sisters. I felt very grown-up and important."

As a teenager, Chakori still feels like it's her job to take care of her little sisters—and her little brother Luke, who was born the year after she and her sisters joined the Redstreet family. "My family always says that we're a three-parent family," Chakori says. "I think that's a good thing most of the time, but sometimes people say I'm too bossy."

Chakori's little sisters seem to be always giggling, but Chakori is more sober. "I have my sad times," she says. "It's not really that I'm sad about anything in particular, it's just this lonely feeling that comes over me. Mom says it's mostly hormones, so maybe it's something I'll outgrow when I'm older. There's really nothing in my life I want to change, so it's not a sadness that really makes any sense."

Chakori still feels connected to her racial heritage. "We live in a community where there are lots of brown people," she explains. "My two best friends are both Indian, though they were born in the United States. Our families like to hang out together, and their moms have taught my mom how to cook real Indian food." The Redstreets have also traveled twice to India. They were unable to locate the girls' biological father, but they visited the orphanage where they stayed. "We came back with suitcases filled with saris and bangles,"

Chakori says. "Mom and the girls and I had such fun shopping."

But mostly Chakori just feels like a Redstreet. "I can't imagine not belonging to this family. Mom, Dad, Luke, Daya, and Prisha—we're a unit. We belong together. That's what a real family is: people who love each other, whose identities and memories are all mixed up together."

She points to her favorite picture of her family. The six people in the photo have different shades of skin—and all wear rose-colored bindis in the center of their foreheads.

What Do You Think?

Why do you think Chakori feels sad sometimes? Do you think she would have been happier growing up in India? Why or why not? What do you think of her definition of a family? How would you define a family?

HEADLINES

(From "Fusion or Confusion: Asian Americans in Multiracial Families" by Todd Lee, Azine, www.aamovement.net/race_identity/fusion1.html)

For Asian Americans raised in multiracial families, the alienation and sense of "otherness" can become a built-in *schizophrenia* of not belonging in either your mother's or father's racial community. In response to this confusion and pain, some children of multiracial families have chosen to visit and/or embrace the home country of their Asian parent or their own original ancestry. This has often produced mixed results. For some, this has been a way to connect to their ancestry and culture and has been helpful and enlightening for them. Others have found that the experience of "going back" has been *alienating* and disappointing. They have sometimes found that the reaction of the native Koreans or Vietnamese or Chinese, etc. has been negative, and that some of the values of the home cultures are *oppressive* or limiting (e.g. the inferior status of women). They have found that as Asian Americans, their American experience and ways have them out of synch with their Asian counterparts, and that among Asians in Asia sometimes they are looked down upon, unable to speak their native language and American in their ways and sensibilities.

These themes: isolation and "otherness" in America and alienation and "otherness" in Asia, seem to point to two things. First, that being Asian American means being a distinct animal—not Asian, not mainstream American, but a *hybrid* experience of a minority in the U.S. And second, that racism and oppression is much of what defines and unites that distinct Asian American experience. While there are certainly some common elements in Asian culture that come from the history

of the region . . . I would argue that the experience I share with Filipino American rappers and Japanese American congressmen has more to do with our experiences facing American racism than a common culture as Asian Americans. The diversity and *complexity* of Asian American culture grows as our immigrant populations increase and the number and diversity of Asians in America also increases. But our *disenfranchisement* from the mainstream culture and society remains. Racism remains, and in a sometimes *perverse* way (e.g. white America's tendency to confuse different Asian nationalities) has united us together in this country. . . . Our continuing experiences, and that of our African American and Latino and Native American brothers and sisters, belie the myth that Dr. King's dream has been achieved. We will not all be "free at last" until the equality that underpins that dream is achieved . . . and we are still a long ways off.

What Do You Think?

How would you describe this author's experience as an Asian adopted into a white American family? Why do you think his experience has been different from Chakori's? Do you think Chakori will eventually face the racism that this author describes as part of his life experience?

The Words We Use

Words shape the world where we live—and in turn, our world shapes the words we use. Sometimes certain words become associated with so much pain and indignity that groups of people choose not to be connected to those words any longer, and instead, they choose new words for themselves, words that will have them claim their identities with pride. But all those different words can be confusing sometimes. Here is a list of some of the words used to describe multiracial families:

African American: A resident or citizen of the United States with African ancestry; many members of this community prefer to be called simply "black."

Afroasian: A person with both African and Asian ancestry.

Amerasian: A resident or citizen of the United States with mixed Asian ancestry. This term includes people who identify as Afroasian, Eurasian, or hapa.

American Indian: A person with Native American ancestry. The term is *controversial* because the label "Indian" is believed to originate with Columbus' mistaken belief he had landed in the South East Asian islands known to Europeans as the Indies. Americans from India do not like this term be used for Native people, while some Native people prefer it.

Amerindian: A person with Native American ancestry.

Anglo: (1) An abbreviation of Anglo American, which comes from Anglo-Saxon (a descendent of the people from the British Islands). (2) In the Southwestern United States, signifies a non-Hispanic European American—a white person.

Asian: (1) A person with ancestors from Asia, an area of the world that includes more than 50 countries or regions. (2) In the United States, the term usually refers to a person with ancestors from Eastern Asia, Southeastern Asia, or Southern Asia. Not usually included in the U.S. usage of this term are Central Asia (former Soviet territories), Northern Asia (Russia), and Western Asia (the Middle East). In the United States, the largest Asian populations are Chinese, Filipino, Indian, Vietnamese, Korean, Japanese, Cambodian, Pakistani, Laotian, Hmong, and Thai.

Asian American: A resident or citizen of the United States with Asian ancestry.

Bicultural: A person who has connections to two different cultures.

Biracial: A person whose biological parents are of two different socially defined races; sometimes considered offensive because of the implication that a biracial person is not complete or whole, and the possible connection to the offensive term "half-breed."

Black: A person with ancestors from Africa.

Caucasian: A person traditionally classified as a member of the Caucasian race, especially a person with light to fair skin. [This definition is no longer in scientific use.] In the United States, this term is often used interchangeably with the term "white." There is a growing movement to discontinue the use of Caucasian and Caucasoid as racial terms, and discard them alongside their archaic partners: Australoid, Mongoloid, and Negroid.

Colored: A person with any amount of non-white ancestry, especially ancestry from Africa; it is an offensive term in the United States.

Eskimo: A person with ancestors from the Native inhabitants of the polar region, excluding Scandinavia and most of Russia. The two main groups are the Inuit and the Yupik. This term is now considered offensive.

Eurasian: A person with both European and Asian ancestry.

European American: A resident or citizen of the United States with European ancestry.

First Nations: A term for the Native people of the Americas, excluding Inuit. Originally used in Canada, now also used in the United States.

Hapa: A person with mixed Asian or Pacific Islander ancestry, from the Hawaiian for "part" or "half." Some Asian transracial adoptees also use this term to identify themselves.

Hispanic: A resident or citizen of the United States with Latin American, Spanish, or Spanish-speaking ancestry. In the United States, the largest Hispanic populations are Mexican, Puerto Rican, Cuban, Salvadoran, Dominican, Guatemalan, Colombian, and Spanish. The term Hispanic is often used interchangeably with the term Latino.

Inuit (plural) / Inuk (singular): A member of one of the indigenous peoples from the Arctic. A native inhabitant of northernmost North America from Northern Alaska to Eastern Canada and Greenland.

Latino/Latina: A resident or citizen of the United Stated with Latin American, Spanish, or Spanish-speaking ancestry. In the United States, the largest Latino populations are Mexican, Puerto Rican, Cuban, Salvadoran, Dominican, Guatemalan, Colombian, and Spanish. Latino is often used interchangeably with the term Hispanic.

Mestizo/Mestiza: A multiracial person, especially in Latin America, with mixed Native American and Spanish (or European) ancestry. Can be considered offensive because the term originated as a preference for lighter skin.

Mulatto: A multiracial person with black and white ancestry; usually a biracial person with one black biological parent and one white biological parent. The word is believed to be derived from the Spanish "mulato" for mule, the infertile crossbreed of a horse and a donkey. Usually considered offensive, although the term has been reclaimed by some people.

Native American: A person with ancestry from the tribes indigenous to the 48 contiguous United States. The largest tribes in the United States today are Navajo, Cherokee, Choctaw, Sioux, Chippewa, Lumbee, Blackfeet, Iroquois, and Pueblo.

Oriental: A term that applies to objects from Asian cultures or countries, such as rugs or furniture. This word does not properly apply to people, and is considered offensive when used to refer to a person with Asian ancestry.

Pacific Islander: A person with ancestry from any of the three regions of Oceania (Polynesia, Micronesia, and Melanesia), including a person with Native Hawaiian, Guamanian or Chamoru, Samoan, Tahitian, or Mariana Islander ancestry.

Person of color: A person with ancestry from the racial or ethnic groups in the United States that historically were or currently are targeted by racism, including people with African, Native American, Asian, or Latino ancestry.

White: (1) A person with European ancestry, often with slight skin pigmentation. (2) As a group, the people who currently have a dominant societal position in the United States.

Find Out More
BOOKS

Alperson, Myra. *Dim Sum, Bagels, and Grits: A Sourcebook for Multicultural Families.* New York: Farrar, Straus & Giroux, 2001.

Frazier, Sundee Tucker. *Check All That Apply: Finding Wholeness as a Multiracial Person.* Downers Grove: Intervarsity Press, 2002.

John, Jaiya. *Black Baby, White Hands: A View From the Crib.* Silver Spring, Md.: Soul Water Rising, 2005.

Nakazawa, Donna Jackson. *Does Anybody Else Look Like Me? A Parent's Guide to Raising Multiracial Children.* Oxford: Perseus, 2003.

Rockquemore, Kerry Ann and Tracey A. Laszloffy. *Raising Biracial Children: From Theory to Practice.* New York: Altimira Press, 2005.

Root, Maria. *Love's Revolution: Interracial Marriage.* Philadelphia: Temple University Press, 2001.

Root, Maria and Matt Kelley. *Multiracial Child Resource Book: Living Complex Identities.* Seattle: MAVIN Foundation, 2003.

Simon, Rita James and Rhonda M. Roorda. *In Their Own Voices: Transracial Adoptees Tell Their Stories.* New York: Columbia University Press, 2000.

Steinberg, Gail and Beth Hall. *Inside Transracial Adoption.* Indianapolis: Perspectives Press, 2000.

Trenka, Jane Jeong, Julia Chinyere Oparah, and Sun Yung Shin, eds. *Outsiders Within: Writing on Transracial Adoption.* Cambridge, Mass.: South End Press, 2006.

Wright, Marguerite A. *I'm Chocolate, You're Vanilla: Raising Healthy Black and Biracial Children in a Race-Conscious World.* San Francisco: Jossey-Bass, 2008.

ON THE INTERNET

Adoptive Families: Transracial Adoptions: The Color of Life
www.adoptivefamilies.com/transracial-adoption.php

Association of MultiEthnic Americans www.ameasite.org

MAVIN Foundation: The Mixed Race Experience
www.mavinfoundation.org

MOSAIC: Equality Knowledge Portal
www.mosaicequalities.org.uk

Multiethnic Education Program
www.multiethniceducation.org

Multiracial Sky: Resources for Multiracial Families
www.multiracialsky.com

Race: Are We So Different?
www.understandingrace.org/home.html

Race: The Power of an Illusion
www.pbs.org/race/000_General/000_00-Home.htm

Swirl: A National Multi-Ethnic Organization
www.swirlinc.org

Bibliography

American Academy of Child & Adolescent Psychiatry. "Facts for Families: Multiracial Children." www.aacap.org/cs/root/facts_for_families/multiracial_children.

Blackmon, J. "Multi-Colored Families: Racially Mixed Households Face Their Own Challenges: Hear How They Are Trying to Meet Them." *Time*. May 3, 1999, p. 80A(1).

Cohn, D, and D. Fears. "Multiracial Growth Seen in Census: Numbers Show Diversity, Complexity of U.S. Count." *The Washington Post*. March 13, 2001 p. A01.

"Color My World: The Promise and Perils of Life in the New Multiracial Mainstream." *Newsweek*. May 8, 2000, p. 70.

"Race: The Power of an Illusion." PBS. www.pbs.org/race/000_General/000_00-Home.htm

ndex

About the Author and the Consultant

AUTHOR

Rae Simons came from a family of five children, and she now has three children of her own. Her role in her "nuclear" family as well as in her extended family continues to shape her life in many ways. As a middle school teacher, she worked closely with a wide range of family configurations. She has written many educational books for young adults.

CONSULTANT

Gallup has studied human nature and behavior for more than seventy years. Gallup's reputation for delivering relevant, timely, and visionary research on what people around the world think and feel is the cornerstone of the organization. Gallup employs many of the world's leading scientists in management, economics, psychology, and sociology, and its consultants assist leaders in identifying and monitoring behavioral economic indicators worldwide. Gallup consultants help organizations boost organic growth by increasing customer engagement and maximizing employee productivity through measurement tools, coursework, and strategic advisory services. Gallup's 2,000 professionals deliver services at client organizations, through the Web, at Gallup University's campuses, and in forty offices around the world.